CAROL VORDERMAN
English Made Easy

10 Minutes A Day

Spelling

Consultant Claire White

Ages
5–7

DK

10-minute challenge

Try to complete the exercises for each topic in 10 minutes or less. Note the time it takes you in the "Time taken" column below.

DK London
Editor Elizabeth Blakemore
Senior Editor Deborah Lock
Managing Editor Christine Stroyan
Managing Art Editor Anna Hall
Consultant Claire White
Senior Production Editor Andy Hilliard
Senior Production Controller Jude Crozier
Jacket Design Development Manager Sophia MTT
Publisher Andrew Macintyre
Associate Publishing Director Liz Wheeler
Art Director Karen Self
Publishing Director Jonathan Metcalf

DK Delhi
Senior Editor Rupa Rao
Editor Rohini Deb
Art Editor Jyotsna
Managing Editors Soma B. Chowdhury, Kingshuk Ghoshal
Managing Art Editor Govind Mittal
Design Consultant Shefali Upadhyay
DTP Designers Anita Yadav, Sachin Gupta, Rakesh Kumar, Harish Aggarwal
Senior Jacket Designer Suhita Dharamjit
Jackets Editorial Coordinator Priyanka Sharma

This edition published in 2020
First published in Great Britain in 2014 by
Dorling Kindersley Limited
DK, One Embassy Gardens, 8 Viaduct Gardens,
London, SW11 7BW

The authorised representative in the EEA is
Dorling Kindersley Verlag GmbH. Arnulfstr. 124,
80636 Munich, Germany

Copyright © 2014, 2020 Dorling Kindersley Limited
A Penguin Random House Company
23 22
022–197387–Apr/2020

A CIP catalogue record for this book
is available from the British Library.
ISBN: 978-1-4093-4142-0

Printed and bound in China

All images © Dorling Kindersley Limited

www.dk.com

MIX
Paper | Supporting responsible forestry
FSC™ C018179

This book was made with Forest Stewardship Council™ certified paper – one small step in DK's commitment to a sustainable future. Learn more at www.dk.com/uk/information/sustainability

Contents

Time taken

Time filler:
In these boxes are some extra challenges to extend your skills. You can do them if you have some time left after finishing the questions. Or, these can be stand-alone activities that you can do in 10 minutes.

Long "a" sound

The letter **a** is often joined with other letters to make this sound. Press the timer and let us get started!

(1) Complete the words with one of these spelling patterns:

ay   ai   a-e

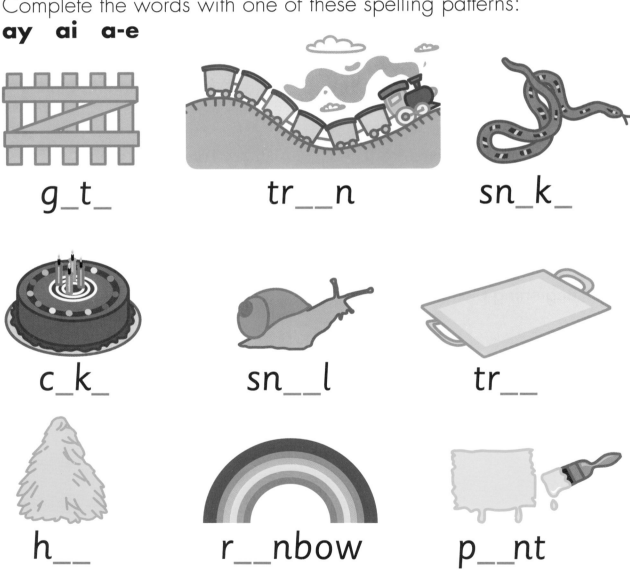

g_t_

tr__n

sn_k_

c_k_

sn__l

tr__

h__

r__nbow

p__nt

(2) Is the **ay** spelling usually at the beginning, in the middle or at the end of a word?

....

Time filler:
Can you say or write
the days of the week?
What is the date of
your birthday?

3 Circle the words with the long "a" sound.

acorn   apple   eight

hat   nail   table

4 Unscramble these letters to find five verbs with the long "a" sound.

ypal   kaem   ebak   twia   tysa

....

5 Complete the words in these sentences. Use **ay**, **ai** or **a-e**.

The tr__l led to a c_v_ and a l_k_.
He couldn't pl__ the g_m_ in the r__n.
The t__l of the wh_l_ m_d_ a spr__.

"ar" and "air" sounds

The letter **a** is joined with other letters to make some other useful vowel sounds. Try them out!

1 Complete these words with the letters **ar** to make the "ar" sound. Use the letters of the alphabet to make words that rhyme.

a b c d e f g h i j k l m n o p q r s t u v w x y z

st__   c__d

sh__k   h__p

__t   f__m

ch__t   __k

j__   y__n

2 Choose a word from the box to complete each sentence.

party	artist	farmer	march

The army went for a ....

The .... rode on a tractor.

Jake put up balloons for his ....

The .... painted a picture.

Time filler:
If you find some words tricky,
you can learn some useful phrases.
To remember "pair" and "pear", learn
this sentence: you feel like you are
walking on AIR in the perfect pAIR of
shoes; a pEAr is a fruit that you EAt.

(3) Say what you see in each picture aloud. Each word has an "air"
sound. This sound can be spelt with the letters **air**, **are** or **ear**.
Use the correct spelling pattern to complete these words.

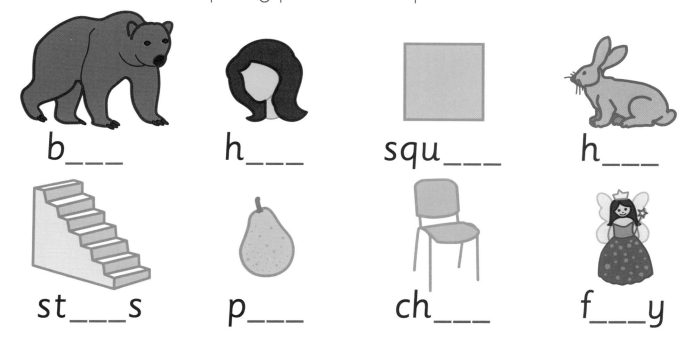

b____   h____   squ____   h____

st____s   p____   ch____   f____y

(4) The spelling pattern **ere** can also make an "air" sound.
Circle the words with this sound in the conversation below.

"Where is the light switch?" asked Jake.

"It is over there by the door," said Jane.

(5) Write two other words that sound like "there",
but are spelt differently.

....

Double letters

Consonants are sometimes doubled after a short vowel sound. Get started and double the letters.

(1) Complete the words by doubling the letter **b**, **d**, **f** or **g**. Join each word to its picture.

a__   ra__it   e__

da__odil   te__y   lu__age

(2) Complete the words by doubling the letter **l**, **m** or **p**. Join each word to its picture.

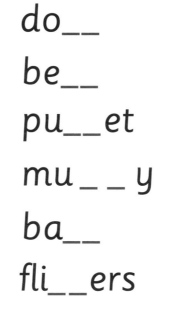

do__
be__
pu__et
mu _ _ y
ba__
fli__ers

Time filler:
Remember the spellings of "desert"
and "dessert" by learning: a deSert
is full of sand with one S and
a deSSert is a pudding full
of Sweet Stuff.

3 Complete the words by doubling the letter **r**, **s** or **t**.
Join each word to its picture.

hi__

a__ow

fo__il

ki__en

che__y

bu__on

4 Complete these words with the letters **ck**.

sa__   ro__et   chi__   ti__et   bu__et

5 Circle the words that **do not** follow the double-letter rule.

off   bus   hid   wall

yes   if   dizzy   cab

Compound words

These words are two or more
words joined together without
changes to their spellings.
Let's find the two words!

1 Join two words to make one word. Then link each to its picture.

hair   fly

butter   house

jelly   brush

light   fish

2 Make six compound words from these words.

race	grand	goal	pop
bed	track	child	hand
keeper	time	corn	shake

....

....

Time filler:
How many words, with two
or more letters, can you make
with the letters in "grandmother"?
Here are three words to get you
started: "moth", "red" and "hand".

(3) Make six compound words, using a word in the red box
and a word in the green box.

| in | out | off | on | up | down |

| doors | side | shoot | going | hill | stairs |

....

....

(4) Split these words into two separate words. Put a line where they split.

bathroom   **firework**   **keyhole**

footprint   **pancake**

(5) How many syllables do these words have?

skyscraper   wheelbarrow   sunshine

newspaper   farmyard   tablespoon

Long "e" sound

The most common spelling patterns
for the long "e" sound are **ee** and **ea**.
Try these pages to see what we mean.

(1) Complete these words with one of these spelling patterns:
ee ea

f__t

__gle

s__ds

s__l

tr__

s__t

(2) Complete each word with the letters **ee**. Then use
the letters of the alphabet to make words that rhyme.

a b c d e f g h i j k l m n o p q r s t u v w x y z

n__d ....

s__k ....

h__l ....

str__t ....

Time filler:
Write about a tree. Try to use lots
of words with the long "e" sound,
such as "leaves", "breeze" and "seeds".
You might like to write a poem!

(3) Complete each word with the letters **ea**. Then use
the letters of the alphabet to make words that rhyme.

a b c d e f g h i j k l m n o p q r s t u v w x y z

n__t ....

l__p ....

cr__m ....

b__st ....

(4) Circle the numbers that have an "ee" sound in the words.

3 6 9 14 18

(5) Use these words to complete the sentences.

seasons teacher week sheep beach

There are seven days in a ....

Tim made a sandcastle on the ....

The .... are spring, summer, autumn and winter.

The field was full of ....

The .... told the class to be quiet.

"ea" or "ear" sounds

The letter **e** is joined with
other letters to make some
other useful vowel sounds.
Get ready, set, go!

(1) Circle the pictures with the short "ea" sound.

eye

head

bread

feather

bird

(2) Add the letters **ea** to complete these words. Say the words aloud.

r__dy   h__vy   thr__d

w__ther   br__kfast   h__lth

(3) Complete the words with one of these spelling patterns:
eer ear

ch___   h___   st___

f___   cl___   d___

Time filler:
To remember the difference between "hear" and "here", learn that you hEAR with your EAR and the position HERE is in tHERE.

4) Use the words you made in question 3 to complete the sentences.

The crowd gave a ....
Dan could .... the crowd.
The fish swam in the .... water.
The people .... the dragon.
" .... the ship to the left," said the captain.
The hikers saw a .... in the forest.

5) Find these words in the word search.

peer   near   deadly   year   already   weapon

s	y	e	o	n	w	d
w	e	a	p	o	n	e
e	a	l	y	r	e	a
c	r	d	a	r	a	d
e	a	p	e	e	r	l
a	l	r	e	a	d	y

Letter clusters

Practise blending two
consonants together at
the end of the word. Letters
cluster together like friends.

1) Add the letters **lp**, **lf** or **lk** to complete these words.

se__   mi__   he__

su__   si__   go__

2) These words end in the letters **lt** or **ld**. Link the words that rhyme.

hold   wild   built   gold

kilt   cold   felt   child

belt
        mild   melt   wilt

3) Choose a word from the box to complete each sentence.

colt	field	shelf	wolf	world

A young horse is called a ....
The book was put on the ....
The .... howled in the night.
The horse galloped around the ....
The news was about people around the ....

Time filler:
Choose 10 words on these pages and put them into alphabetical order. Here are the letters of the alphabet to help you:
a b c d e f g h i j k l m
n o p q r s t u v w x y z

④ Read the words on the coins. Then sort these words into sets by writing them on the piggy banks.

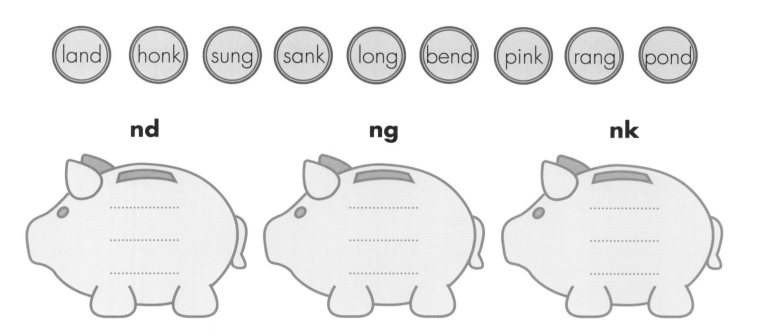

nd

ng

nk

⑤ Change the vowel in each of these verbs to write what happened yesterday and what will have happened by tomorrow.

Today	Yesterday (change vowel to **a**)	Tomorrow (change vowel to **u**)
sing		
ring		
sink		
drink		

Verb endings

Add -**ed** or -**ing** to
the end of a verb to tell
when something happens.
Let us get started!

1 Add -**ing** to each verb to tell what is happening now.

shout___   lift___   cook___

pull___   jump___   rest___

2 Add -**ed** to each verb to tell what has happened before.

melt__   ask__   help__

land__   climb__   look__

3 These verbs end in **e**. Drop the **e** in these verbs
before adding -**ing** or -**ed**.

Verb	Happen**ing** now (add -**ing**)	Happen**ed** before (add -**ed**)
use		
bake		
hike		
vote		

Time filler:
Make a list of everything you have done today. Circle the verbs. What ending have you used to write about your day?

4) Tick (✔) the correct spelling.

☐ ☐
marryed or married

☐ ☐
marrying or marriing

☐ ☐
cryed or cried

☐ ☐
crying or criing

☐ ☐
enjoyed or enjoied

☐ ☐
enjoying or enjoiing

Write the rule for when a **y** is changed to an **i**.

....

5) These verbs have a short vowel sound. Double the last consonant before adding the verb endings -**ing** and -**ed** to each word.

fit [add -**ing**] ⟶ ....

spot [add -**ed**] ⟶ ....

hum [add -**ing**] ⟶ ....

tap [add -**ed**] ⟶ ....

cut [add -**ing**] ⟶ ....

rub [add -**ed**] ⟶ ....

Useful word list 1

Read each column of words. After that, cover the words up word by word and write them. Then move on to the next column.

he		have		can	
she		has		say	
him		had		said	
his		here		with	
her		came		want	
you		come		was	
me		some		will	
my		see		well	
are		saw		went	
for		how		were	

Time filler:
Choose five words in this list and use each one in its own sentence. Keep coming back to these lists to check that you still know these useful words.

one	the	made
two	that	make
did	they	more
do	their	much
down	them	why
up	then	where
so	this	when
no	there	which
new	these	who
now	three	what

More clusters

Listen out for consonants
that have their own sounds,
but blend with other
consonants in words.

1 Add the letters **sp**, **sk** or **xt** to complete these words.

ga__   ma__   ne__

de__   te__   cri__

2 These words end with the letters **nt** or **st**. Link the words that rhyme.

last   bent   nest   dent

list   fist   past

fast   mist

west   tent   best

3 Choose a word from the box to complete each sentence.

left   stamp   gift   tent   beast

Todd and Sammy slept in a ....

The .... had sharp teeth and hooked claws.

Turn .... at the roundabout.

I wrapped my .... for Dad's birthday.

A .... goes on an envelope.

Time filler:
How many words, with
two or more letters, can
you make with the letters
in "breakfast"? Here are two
words to get you started:
"star" and "ask".

④ Read the words on the coins. Then sort these words
into sets by writing them on the piggy banks.

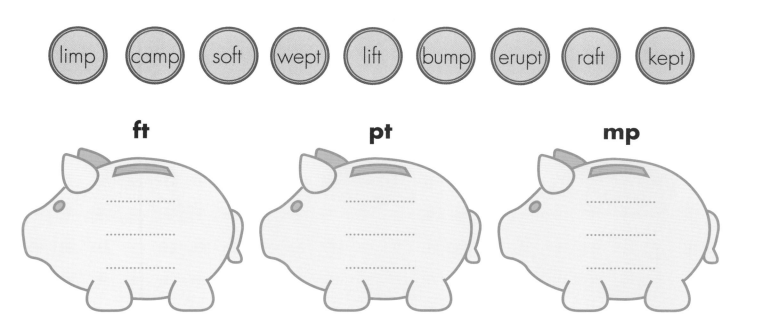

limp   camp   soft   wept   lift   bump   erupt   raft   kept

ft

pt

mp

⑤ Find these words in the word search.

grasp   jump   crept   post   wrist   stump

t	g	r	a	s	p
p	r	a	j	t	c
o	u	j	u	s	r
s	t	u	m	p	e
t	l	g	p	m	p
s	w	r	i	s	t

24

"er" sound

The "er" sound has many spelling patterns, such as **er**, **ir** and **ur**, so choose carefully.

1 Complete the words with one of these spelling patterns:
er   ir   ur

f __ __ n

b __ __ d

lant __ __ n

p __ __ se

t __ __ tle

sk __ __ t

2 Unscramble these letters to find five nouns with the "er" sound.

hrtist   ilgr   rekuty   vruce   dreh

....

3 These names of jobs end with the letters **er**. Complete the words.

teach __ __   farm __ __   danc __ __

driv __ __   build __ __   lawy __ __

Time filler:
To remember how to spell "together", split it into **TO GET HER** and then you will be **TOGETHER**. Or try splitting it up into sound chunks: to-geth-er. Try splitting these words up into chunks: "wonderful" and "different".

(4) Read the words. Draw a picture to show the meaning of each word.

stir

squirt

dirty

burn

burst

shatter

(5) Complete the words in these sentences, using **er**, **ir** or **ur**.

I grew some mint in the h__b patch.

Jake took photos with his cam__a.

The b__ds whistled and ch__ped.

Blends and ends

Consonant letter blends can appear at the beginning, in the middle or at the end of a word. Listen out for them.

1 Look at the pictures. Add the letters **sh** or **ch** to complete the words.

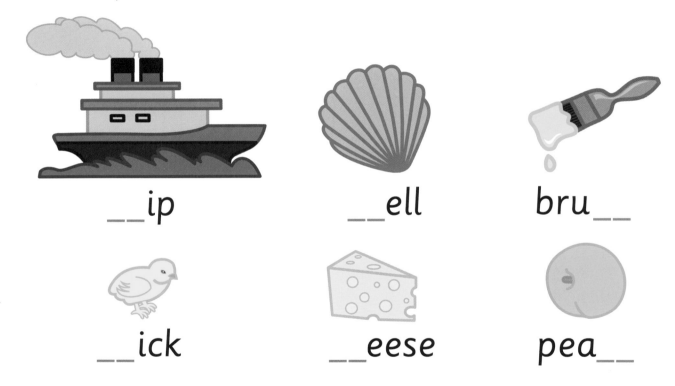

__ip   __ell   bru__

__ick   __eese   pea__

2 Underline the "th" sound when it appears in these sentences.
Note: There are two "th" sounds as in "then" and in "thistle".

The three brothers were thrilled.

Thunder crashed around them.

Their mother and father were thankful.

Time filler:
Try saying this tongue twister:
Chester chews through shoes.
Should Chester choose the shoes
he chews? Make your own tongue
twister with the **ch**, **sh** and **th** letters.

3 Draw a line to link the words that rhyme.

match   lunch   fish   catch

bunch   hatch   cash   wish

dash   munch   dish

sash

4 Change the vowel sound to make a new word from each of these words. Use **a**, **e**, **i**, **o** or **u**.

think   shop   rush   bench   hutch

....

5 Complete these words using the letters **shr** or **thr**.

___one   ___ub   ___ob

___imp   ___oat   ___iek

Compare adjectives

Adjectives describe people, places or things. Add **-er** or **-est** to compare them.

① Add **-er** to each word to compare two things.

fast__   rich__   weak__

slow__   poor__   strong__

② Add **-est** to each word to mean the top thing.

old___   low___   short___

young___   high___   tall___

③ These words have a short vowel sound.
Double the last consonant before adding the endings.

Adjective	Compare two things (add -**er**)	The top things (add -**est**)
fit		
thin		
hot		
wet		

Time filler:
Compare the members of your family and set some challenges. Who is the tallest, or who runs the fastest? Is there anyone smaller than you? Can you hop for longer, and who can jump the highest?

4) These words end in **e** or **y**. Drop the **e** or change the **y** to an **i** in these words before adding -**er** or -**est**.

nice [add -**er**] → ....   pretty [add -**est**] → ....

wide [add -**er**] → ....   large [add -**est**] → ....

heavy [add -**er**] → ....   tiny [add -**est**] → ....

5) Some adjectives do not follow the rules. Use these words to complete the chart.

| little | better | worst | many | most | less |

Adjective	Compare two things	The top things
good		best
		least
bad	worse	
	more	

Long "i" sound

The letter **i** often joins with other letters to form the long "i" sound. But the letter **y** makes the sound, too.

(1) Complete these words with one of these spelling patterns:
ie   **i-e**

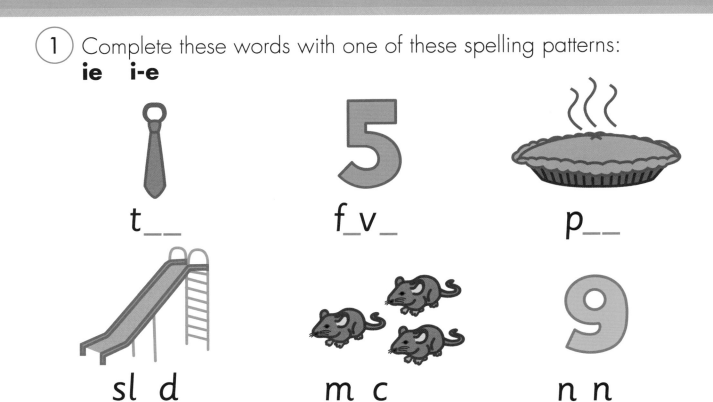

t_ _

f_v_

p_ _

sl_d_

m_c_

n_n_

(2) Unscramble the letters to make words with the letter **y** as the long "i" sound.

yrc   yub   yfl   syk   yrt

....

(3) Complete the words in these sentences, using **igh**, **i-e**, **y** or **ie**.

The br___t star sh_n_s in the n___t sk_.

The k_t_ fl__s h___ and d_v_s low.

Time filler:
Write about night time. Try to use
lots of words with the long "i" sound,
such as "moonlight", "sky" and "fireflies".
You might like to write a poem!

4) Read the words on the bows. Then sort these words into sets
of the same spelling patterns and write them on the kites.

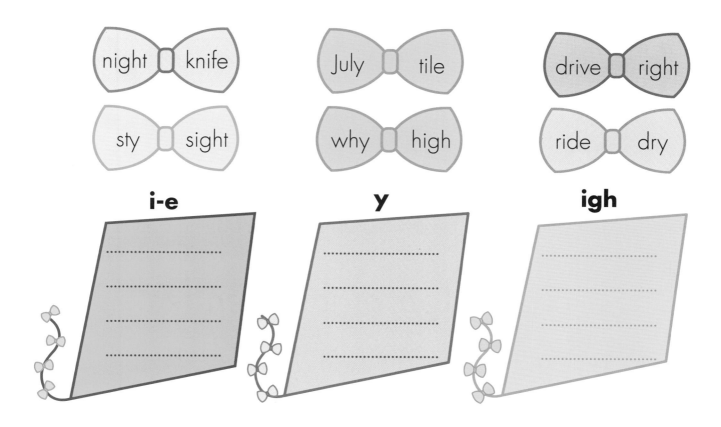

night | knife

July | tile

drive | right

sty | sight

why | high

ride | dry

i-e

y

igh

5) Complete these words with the long "i" sound. Then use
the letters of the alphabet to make words that rhyme.

a b c d e f g h i j k l m n o p q r s t u v w x y z

p_l_ ....

l_k_ ....

f_r_ ....

w_s_ ....

Beginning blends

Here are some more
consonant clusters at
the beginning of a word.

(1) Use these beginning blends to complete the words below:

cl   pl   sl

__ock

__ant

__ide

(2) In each sentence, circle the blends **bl** and **cl** at the start of words.

The black blob of ink blended
on the blot.

The broken clock went clink,
clank, clunk.

(3) Unscramble these letters to find five words beginning
with either **gl** or **pl**.

dgal   napl   tolp   geul   spul

....

Time filler:
Look at the letters on car number plates. Think of words with those letters in them. For example, a registration PAM could make "palm" and "stamp".

(4) Use these beginning blends to complete the words:
br   dr   fr   gr   pr   tr

__og   __ass   __um

__ize   __uck   __ick

(5) Read the words on the bricks. Then sort these words into sets by writing them on the walls.

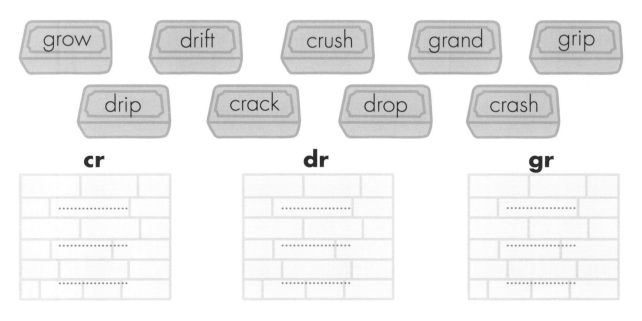

grow   drift   crush   grand   grip

drip   crack   drop   crash

cr   **dr**   **gr**

Contractions

When words combine and drop
letters, an apostrophe is used to
show that letters are missing.
Are you ready to try these?

(1) Separate each word into two words.

he's   ....

you'll   ....

didn't   ....

I've   ....

(2) Combine the two words to make one word in each case.

can not   ....

you are   ....

she will   ....

we have   ....

(3) Match each pair of words to its contraction.

could not   don't

do not   it's

I am   I'm

it is   couldn't

Time filler:
Look through comics, magazines and books and point out the contractions. What effect do the contractions have on the way the words are spoken?

4 For each sentence, circle the two words that can be combined. Write the contraction.

Who is coming to see the movie? ....

You are going to be late for the show. ....

What is on today? ....

We have been to the cinema. ....

5 Tick (✔) the correct sentences and put a cross (✗) against an error. Then correct the mistakes.

"Where's your book?" asked the teacher. ☐ ....

"Its at home," said Emma. ☐ ....

She'ad forgotten it. ☐ ....

"I'll bring it in tomorrow," she said. ☐ ....

Long "o" sound

The letter **o** often joins other letters to make spelling patterns for the long "o" sound. Off you go!

1) Complete these words with one of these spelling patterns:
oa   oe   o-e   ow

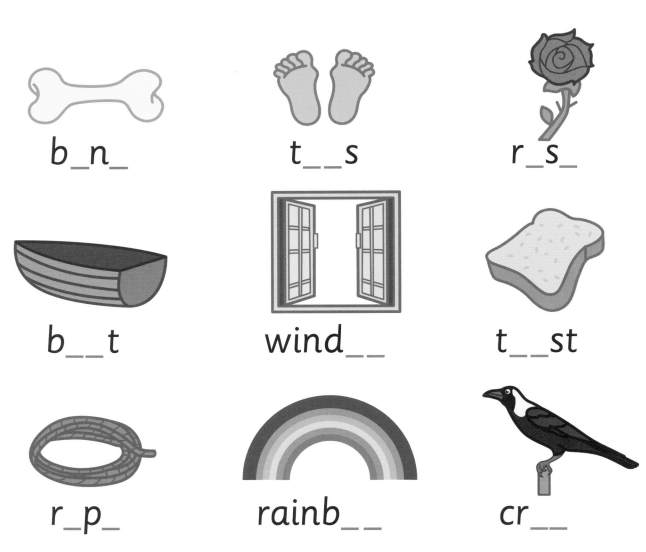

b _ n _   t _ _ s   r _ s _

b _ _ t   wind _ _   t _ _ st

r _ p _   rainb _ _   cr _ _

2) Is the **ow** spelling for the long "o" sound used at the beginning, in the middle or at the end of a word?

....

Time filler:
A useful way to know the spelling of some tricky words is to learn a phrase that uses the letters in order. For example, for the word "ocean", remember "Only Cats' Eyes Are Narrow". Make your own phrases for words that you find tricky to spell.

3) Complete each word with the letters **oa**. Then use the letters of the alphabet to make words that rhyme with each one.

a b c d e f g h i j k l m n o p q r s t u v w x y z

s__k ....

c__ch ....

fl__t ....

c__st ....

4) Circle the words with the long "o" sound.

soap   cow   hoe   globe

5) Unscramble these letters to find five verbs with the long "o" sound.

keow   obwl   dola   rogw   kroca

"oy" and "ow" sounds

Here are some more useful spelling patterns to know and use. How well will you do?

① Circle the pictures with the "oy" and "ow" sounds.

② Add the letters **oi** to complete these words. Say the words aloud.

b__l   p__nt   n__sy

c__n   v__ce   s__l

③ Complete these words with one of these spelling patterns:
oi   oy

j__n   t__   enj__

ann__   ch__ce   r__al

Time filler:
Go outside and make some noisy
sounds: "howl", "growl" and "oink".
What other noises do animals make?
Listen out for the vowel sounds in these
words: "chirp", "screech" and "croak".

4) Complete each word with the letters **ou** or **ow**. Then use the
letters of the alphabet to make words that rhyme with each one.
a b c d e f g h i j k l m n o p q r s t u v w x y z

cr _ _ n ....

all _ _ ....

m _ _ th ....

cl _ _ d ....

h _ _ l ....

h _ _ se ....

fl _ _ er ....

f _ _ nd ....

5) Use these words to complete the sentences below.

| loud | down | mouse | outside | crowd |

The .... gave a cheer and waved flags.

The music was very .... at the concert.

A lady screamed when she saw a ....

The people went .... the stairs.

When it started to rain ...., everyone ran inside.

Tricky blends

In some consonant blends,
it is tricky to hear each letter.
Watch out as you try these.

① Complete these words by adding the letters **wh** or **tw**.

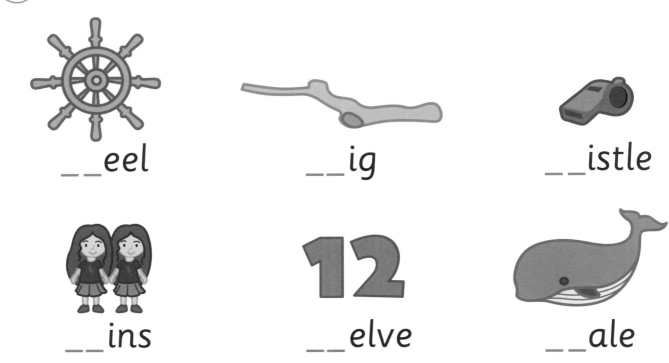

__eel

__ig

__istle

__ins

__elve

__ale

② Use these words to complete the sentences.

twenty	twinkled	quicker	tweezers	twisted

I pick up the stamp with ....

The vines grew and .... around the fence.

The stars were bright and .... in the sky.

.... is written with the digits 2 and 0.

A cheetah is .... than an elephant.

3 Match each question to its word answer.

What noise does a duck make? quill

What did ancient writers use to write?   queen

What is a king's wife called? quiet

What is the opposite of noisy?  quack

4 Circle the letters that make the "f" sound in these words.

elephant telephone dolphin

5 Which two letters make the "f" sound? ....

Which two letters make the "kw" sound? ....

Plurals

A plural is more than one
of something. Let us change
one thing to more than one.

1) Most words are made plural by adding an **s**, but there are
exceptions. If the ending has an extra syllable, then add **-es**.
Write the plural forms for these words.

cat .... box ....

rock .... glass ....

2) Tick (✔) the spelling that is right.

☐ ☐   ☐ ☐

    valleys or valleies   ladys or ladies

☐ ☐   ☐ ☐

    citys or cities   pennys or pennies

☐ ☐   ☐ ☐

    keys or keies   chimneys or chimneies

Write the rule for when a **y** is changed to an **i**.

....

3) If a word ends in an "f" sound, change the **f** to a **v** and add **-es**.
Write the plural forms for these words.

knife   shelf   calf   leaf

....

Time filler:
Find ten objects around your home. Use a dictionary to spell their plural forms. What spelling patterns have you used?

4 Make the words plural by adding **-s** or **-es**. Check in a dictionary.

kangaroo ....

piano ....

hero ....

tomato ....

potato ....

volcano ....

5 Some words change completely from the singular to the plural form. Match each word to its correct plural.

 goose

children

 tooth

geese

 child

mice

 mouse

teeth

Useful word list 2

Read each column of words. After that, cover the words up word by word and write them. Then move on to the next column.

left	....	boy	....
right	....	girl	....
last	....	before	....
first	....	after	....
second	....	again	....
third	....	always	....
fast	....	own	....
slow	....	found	....
four	....	round	....
five	....	good	....

Time filler:
Choose five words in this list and use each one in its own sentence. Keep coming back to these lists to check that you still know these useful words.

any	....	red	....
only	....	black	....
ask	....	blue	....
put	....	white	....
pull	....	green	....
push	....	brown	....
than	....	yellow	....
thing	....	grey	....
think	....	purple	....
thought	....	orange	....

"or" sound

Practise spelling words with the "or" sound, as in sh**or**t and in p**au**se. Let us go!

---

1 Complete these words with one of these spelling patterns:

or   oar   oor   ore

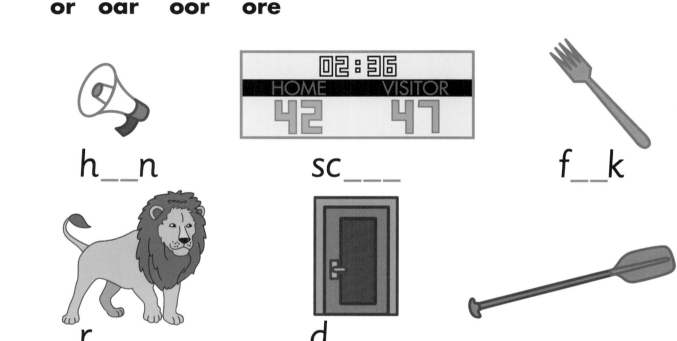

h__n

02:36
HOME   VISITOR
42   47

sc____

f__k

r____

d____

____

---

2 Unscramble these letters to find five words with the "or" sound.

arro   reom   norb   trof   rlofo

....

---

3 Complete these words with the spelling patterns **au** or **aw**.

cl__   sh__l   __thor

p__print   str__   s__cer

47

Time filler:
Here is a phrase to help you
spell "because": Big Elephants Can
Always Understand Small Elephants.
Write a sentence with "because" in it.

4 Find these words in the word search.

board   wore   crawl   sport   north   dawn

t	w	d	c	s	n
b	o	a	r	d	o
o	r	w	a	s	r
s	e	n	w	p	t
t	h	g	l	m	h
s	p	o	r	t	t

5 Use these words to complete the sentences below.

haunted   drawer   fork   corners

Everybody was scared to go into the _____ house.

A triangle has three _____.

Liz put away her shirts in the top _____.

His _____ slipped off his plate.

More beginning blends

The letter **s** starts many consonant blends, especially at the beginning of a word.

1 Read the words on the stamps. Then sort these words into sets by writing them on the envelopes.

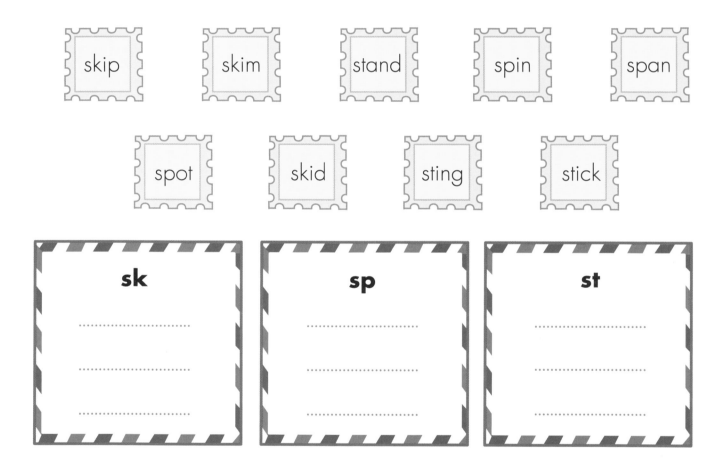

skip   skim   stand   spin   span

spot   skid   sting   stick

sk

....

....

....

sp

....

....

....

st

....

....

....

2 Complete each word with one of these blends: **sc   sl   sw   sm**

__ an   __ arf   __ ing

__ ell   __ ift   __ ile

Time filler:
Try saying this tongue twister:
Shirley slept sweetly.
Use the words on these pages and others, you can think of, to make your own tongue twister. Use words with the letters **sk, sp** and **st**.

3) Circle the letter that has changed each time.

smell — spell — spill — still — stilt

snip — skip — slip — slim — skim

4) Complete each word using the letter blends **spr**, **str** or **scr**. Then use the letters of the alphabet to make words that rhyme.
a b c d e f g h i j k l m n o p q r s t u v w x y z

___int   ....   ___uff   ....

___and   ....   ___ong   ....

5) Match each question to its word answer.

What does an actor use?   swim

What is the noise of
a ball falling in water?   script

How does a fish move
about in water?   splash

Long "oo" sound

Listen carefully for the
"oo" sound as in m**oo**n.
Watch out, as the "oo" sound is
often made with different letters.

1) Circle the words with the long "oo" sound.

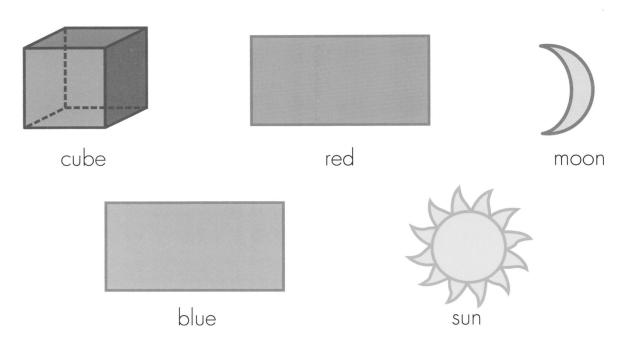

cube   red   moon

blue   sun

2) Complete these words with one of these spelling patterns:
oo ew u-e

fl_t_   gr_ _   f_ _d

fl_ _   n_ _t   bl_ _

3) Unscramble these letters to find five words with the long "oo" sound.

eluc   neut   toro   retwh   eugh

....

Time filler:
Here is a phrase to help you spell "beautiful": Big Ears Aren't Ugly, they're BEAUtiful. Make a phrase for the word "queue", beginning with "Queen Una."

4) Complete each word using the letters **oo** or **ue**.
Then use the letters of the alphabet to make words that rhyme.
a b c d e f g h i j k l m n o p q r s t u v w x y z

f__d ....   r__t ....

gl__ ....   d__ ....

s__n ....   br__m ....

z__ ....   h__p ....

t__l ....   arg__ ....

5) Choose a word from the box to complete the sentences below.

| hoop | blue | broom | true |

A .... balloon floated in the sky.

The dog jumped through the ....

The statement, "The blue whale is the largest mammal," is ....

Cinderella used a .... to sweep the floor.

Short "oo" sound

This "oo" sound is in **foo**t and p**u**sh. The sound mostly appears in the middle of a word.

(1) The letters **oo** are used to spell two different sounds. Circle the pictures with the short **oo** sound.

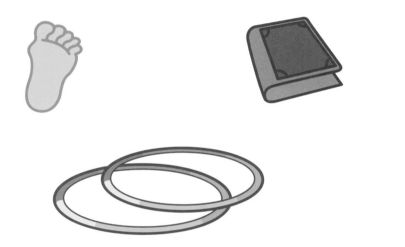

(2) Complete these words with the **oo** spelling.

l__k   st__d   w__d

br__k   t__k   w__l

(3) Write a sentence for each of these words.

could   ....

should   ....

would   ....

Time filler:
Here is a way to help you
remember how to spell
"could", "would" and "should".
Write the initial sound
then think, "O U Lucky Duck!"

4) Find these words in the word search.

shook   hood   good   cook   soot

brook   foot   wood   crook   book

s	g	c	a	z	i	e
h	o	o	d	f	c	y
o	o	o	u	o	r	p
o	d	k	w	o	o	d
k	s	o	o	t	o	q
j	b	r	o	o	k	a
b	o	o	k	w	e	m

5) Use the letter **u** to make the short "oo" sound in each word.

p_ll   p_sh   s_gar

b_sh   f_ll   b_ll

Silent letters

In some words, certain letters are silent! They are there but you can't hear them when you say the word. See if you can spot them!

1 Match each picture to the letters its word begins with.

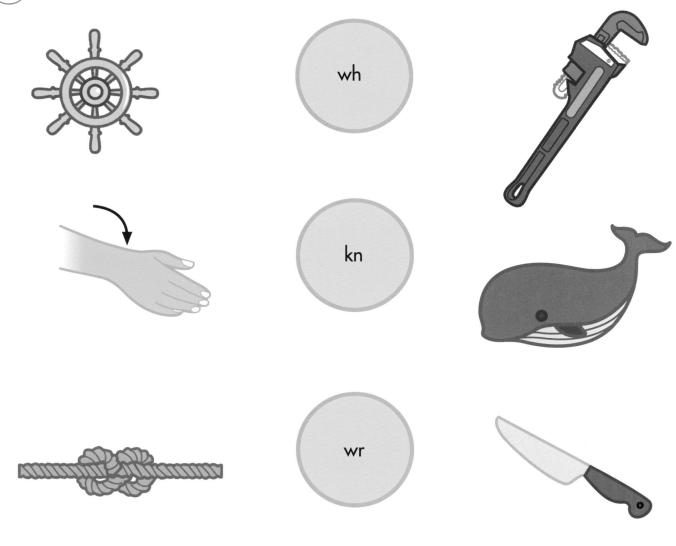

wh

kn

wr

2 Underline the letters that are silent in these words.

knit   wrist   guard   sign

write   wrap   knee   knife

Time filler:
Here is a phrase to help you spell "Wednesday": WE Do Not Eat Soup on WEDNESdays. How many words, with two or more letters, can you make with the letters in Wednesday?

3 Use the letter blends **mn** or **mb** to complete these words.

hy_ _   cli_ _   la_ _

colu_ _   thu _ _   autu_ _

4 Use these words to complete the sentences.

| wrong | guests | kneels | crumbs | castle |

The priest _____ to pray.

Jen gave the _____ from the bread to the birds.

The _____ is a splendid building.

The answer was _____ and marked with a cross.

The hotel had room for 50 _____ .

5 Underline the silent letters in these words.

wriggle   wreath   knock

whistle   guitar   island

Prefixes and suffixes

A prefix is a part of a word added to its beginning and a suffix, to its end. They change the word's meaning.

① Add the prefix **un-** to the beginning of each of these words.

__happy   __do   __load

__fair   __lock   __well

What do you think the prefix **un-** means? ....

② Add the suffix -**less** to the ends of these words.

hope____   rest____   end____

tire____   speech____   age____

What do you think the suffix -**less** means? ....

③ Complete these words.

enjoy + ment = ...   sad + ness = ...

punish + ment = ...   fit + ness = ...

agree + ment = ...   dark + ness = ...

pay + ment = ...   ill + ness = ...

Time filler:
Use a dictionary to find the meanings of five words on these pages. How has the prefix or suffix changed each word's meaning?

(4) Add the suffix **-ful** to the ends of these words.

use___   cheer___   pain___

wonder___   care___   mind___

What do you think the suffix **-ful** means? ....

(5) Combine a word from the red box with a word part from the green box to make 10 new words.

| joy   play   glad   open   help   power   cover |

| un-   -less   -ful   -ness |

Count the syllables for each of your new words.

.... ☐   .... ☐

.... ☐   .... ☐

.... ☐   .... ☐

.... ☐   .... ☐

The letter **y**

Watch out for the letter **y** as it makes different letter sounds. Have a try!

① The letter **y** sometimes makes a long "e" sound at the end of a word. Add a **y** to complete these words.

bab_

famil_

hone_

② The letter **y** makes a long "i" sound when there are no other vowels in the word. Unscramble these letters to make words.

kys   yhw   rcy   ylf   ryf

....

③ Tick (✔) in the correct box to show what sound the **y** makes.

Word	Long "e" sound	Long "i" sound
body		
type		
empty		
shy		

4 The letter **y** can also make a long "a" sound and a short "i" sound. Find these words in the word search.

prey   cylinder   pyramid   syrup   crystal   myth   gym

s	p	h	t	g	y	m	c
c	y	l	i	n	d	e	r
p	r	e	y	u	t	s	y
d	a	y	m	a	h	p	s
l	m	s	y	r	u	p	t
y	i	p	t	h	a	y	a
c	d	l	h	t	y	g	l

5 For plurals, if the **y** follows a consonant, then change the **y** to an **i** and add -**es**. Tick (✔) the correct plural.

☐   ☐
babys or babies

☐   ☐
monkeys or monkeies

☐   ☐
trays or traies

☐   ☐
familys or families

"j" and "l" sounds

Some consonant sounds have more than one spelling pattern.

① The letter **j** is never used at the end of a word. Instead, the "j" sound is spelt with -**dge** after the short vowel sounds and -**ge** after all other sounds. Complete these words using the spelling patterns **dge** or **ge**.

ca__   bri___   he___

② Complete these words with **dge** or **ge**.
Then use the words to fill in the sentences.

hu__   char__   le___   fu___   villa__

The bird sat on the window ....

Who is the person in ....?

The baker made a .... birthday cake flavoured with ....

Everyone in the .... was excited about the mayor's visit.

3 Often when the "j" sound comes before **e**, **i** or **y**, the letter **g** is used. Complete these words using **j** or **g**.

_em   _uice   _iraffe   _am

4 The "l" sound at the end of a word has either an -**le** or -**el** spelling. Tick (✔) the words that have been spelt correctly.

☐ single   ☐ jungel   ☐ parcel   ☐ simpel

☐ towle   ☐ label   ☐ kennel   ☐ candle

5 Complete these words with -**al** or -**il**.

penc__   sand__   utens__

anim__   foss__   pet__

Homophones and homographs

Make sure you pay attention because some words can be very similar.

(1) Homophones are words that sound the same but are spelt differently. Link the homophones.

won   see   I   write   red   hear

right   here   sea   one   eye   read

(2) Complete the sentences using these words.

| to | too | two | there | their | they're |

A letter was sent .... the man.

.... were .... trees in the garden.

The children read .... books.

The teacher read her book, ...

.... reading about monkeys.

(3) Draw two pictures for each word.

bat

glasses

bark

Time filler:
Design your own homophone poster with drawings for these words: "meat" and "meet", "one" and "won", and "blue" and "blew".

(4) Two words that are spelt the same but have different meanings are called homographs. Look at the words in the box. Write them under the pictures.

| ring | bowl | match | sink |

....

....

(5) Write the homophone under each picture.

| blew | hair | night | which |

witch

knight

blue

hare

....

Useful word list 3

Read each column of words. After that, cover the words up word by word and write them. Then move on to the next column.

could	....	Monday	....
should	....	Tuesday	....
would	....	Wednesday	....
very	....	Thursday	....
every	....	Friday	....
other	....	Saturday	....
another	....	Sunday	....
because	....	today	....
open	....	tomorrow	....
close	....	yesterday	....

Time filler:
Choose five words in this list and use each one in its own sentence. Keep coming back to these lists to check that you still know these useful words.

January	November	
February	December	
March	month	
April	year	
May	school	
June	rain	
July	cloud	
August	snow	
September	wind	
October	weather	

66

Answers:

04–05 Long "a" sound
06–07 "ar" and "air" sounds

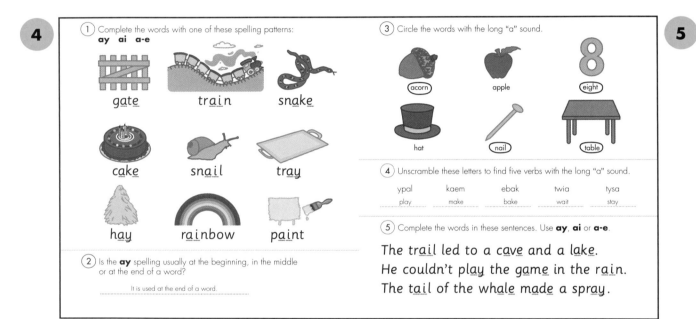

4

① Complete the words with one of these spelling patterns:
ay   ai   a-e

gate   tr<u>ai</u>n   sn<u>a</u>k<u>e</u>

cake   sn<u>ai</u>l   tr<u>ay</u>

h<u>ay</u>   r<u>ai</u>nbow   p<u>ai</u>nt

② Is the **ay** spelling usually at the beginning, in the middle or at the end of a word?

It is used at the end of a word.

5

③ Circle the words with the long "a" sound.

(acorn)   apple   (eight)

hat   (nail)   (table)

④ Unscramble these letters to find five verbs with the long "a" sound.

ypal   kaem   ebak   twia   tysa
play   make   bake   wait   stay

⑤ Complete the words in these sentences. Use **ay**, **ai** or **a-e**.

The tr<u>ai</u>l led to a c<u>a</u>v<u>e</u> and a l<u>a</u>k<u>e</u>.
He couldn't pl<u>ay</u> the g<u>a</u>m<u>e</u> in the r<u>ai</u>n.
The t<u>ai</u>l of the wh<u>a</u>l<u>e</u> m<u>a</u>d<u>e</u> a spr<u>ay</u>.

By this stage, children should be able to distinguish between hearing long and short vowel sounds and be aware that the long vowel sounds are represented by more than one spelling pattern. These pages reinforce three of the most frequently used spelling patterns representing the long "a" sound, including the vowel and a final -**e**. Point out to your child that "eight" uses completely different letters for the long "a" sound.

6

① Complete these words with the letters **ar** to make the "ar" sound. Use the letters of the alphabet to make words that rhyme.
a b c d e f g h i j k l m n o p q r s t u v w x y z

Rhyming words will vary.

st<u>ar</u>   car   c<u>ar</u>d   hard

sh<u>ar</u>k   bark   h<u>ar</u>p   sharp

<u>ar</u>t   part   f<u>ar</u>m   harm

ch<u>ar</u>t   start   <u>ar</u>k   lark

j<u>ar</u>   far   y<u>ar</u>n   barn

② Choose a word from the box to complete each sentence.

| party | artist | farmer | march |

The army went for a ....march........
The ....farmer........ rode on a tractor.
Jake put up balloons for his ....party........ .
The ....artist........ painted a picture.

7

③ Say what you see in each picture aloud. Each word has an "air" sound. This sound can be spelt with the letters **air**, **are** or **ear**. Use the correct spelling pattern to complete these words.

b<u>ear</u>   h<u>air</u>   squ<u>are</u>   h<u>are</u>

st<u>air</u>s   p<u>ear</u>   ch<u>air</u>   f<u>air</u>y

④ The spelling pattern **ere** can also make an "air" sound. Circle the words with this sound in the conversation below.

"(Where) is the light switch?" asked Jake.
"It is over (there) by the door," said Jane.

⑤ Write two other words that sound like "there", but are spelt differently.

........they're........   ....their........

Children should know that in the majority of words every syllable must have a vowel sound. They may now begin to recognise the use of other common vowel sounds, such as "ar" and "air". Just as for other vowel sounds, there are often more than one spelling pattern, and these are practised on these green pages.

Answers:

08–09 Double letters
10–11 Compound words

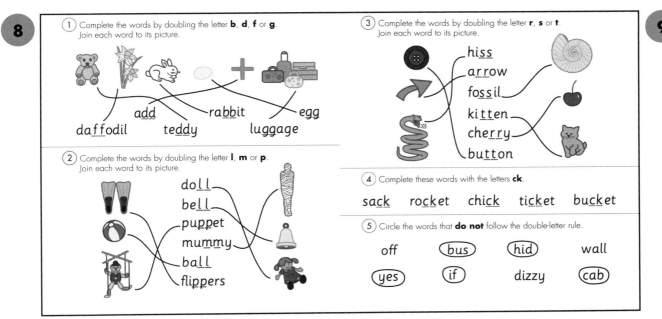

8

1) Complete the words by doubling the letter **b**, **d**, **f** or **g**. Join each word to its picture.

add   rabbit   egg
daffodil   teddy   luggage

2) Complete the words by doubling the letter **l**, **m** or **p**. Join each word to its picture.

doll
bell
puppet
mummy
ball
flippers

9

3) Complete the words by doubling the letter **r**, **s** or **t**. Join each word to its picture.

hiss
arrow
fossil
kitten
cherry
button

4) Complete these words with the letters **ck**.

sack   rocket   chick   ticket   bucket

5) Circle the words that **do not** follow the double-letter rule.

off   (bus)   (hid)   wall
(yes)   (if)   dizzy   (cab)

Ask children to say words and listen for the vowel sound to extend their awareness of when some consonants are doubled. They will notice the short "a", "e", "i", "o" or "u" sound just before the doubled consonant. You may also like to point out the sound **o** makes in "daffodil" and "arrow". Encourage children to notice words with doubled letters. They will see that the letters **f**, **l**, **s** and **z** are doubled at the end of words.

10

1) Join two words to make one word. Then link each to its picture.

hair   fly
butter   house
jelly   brush
light   fish

2) Make six compound words from these words.

race	grand	goal	pop
bed	track	child	hand
keeper	time	corn	shake

racetrack   grandchild   goalkeeper
bedtime   popcorn   handshake

11

3) Make six compound words, using a word in the red box and a word in the green box. Answers may vary.

| in | out | off | on | up | down |

| doors | side | shoot | going | hill | stairs |

indoors   outside   downstairs
offshoot   uphill   ongoing

4) Split these words into two separate words. Put a line where they split.

bath|room   fire|work   key|hole
foot|print   pan|cake

5) How many syllables do these words have?

| skyscraper | wheelbarrow | sunshine |
| 3 | 3 | 2 |

| newspaper | farmyard | tablespoon |
| 3 | 2 | 3 |

Children often enjoy joining complete words together to make compound words or finding where the two words split. A useful spelling tip is to break long words into syllables and then work out the spelling of these more manageable chunks of letters. Encourage children to clap the syllables as they say the words to help identify how many syllables there are. Ask children to think of other compound words they may be familiar with and point them out during your conversations.

Answers:

12-13 Long "e" sound
14-15 "ea" and "ear" sounds

12

1. Complete these words with one of these spelling patterns: **ee ea**

feet eagle seeds

seal tree seat

2. Complete each word with the letters **ee**. Then use the letters of the alphabet to make words that rhyme.
abcdefghijklmnopqrstuvwxyz
Rhyming words will vary.

need — seed   seek — creek

heel — reel   street — beat

13

3. Complete each word with the letters **ea**. Then use the letters of the alphabet to make words that rhyme.
abcdefghijklmnopqrstuvwxyz
Rhyming words will vary.

neat — feet   leap — keep

cream — steam   beast — feast

4. Circle the numbers that have an "ee" sound in the words.

③ 6 9 ⑭ ⑱

5. Use these words to complete the sentences.

seasons teacher week sheep beach

There are seven days in a ___week___
Tim made a sandcastle on the ___beach___.
The ___seasons___ are spring, summer, autumn and winter.
The field was full of ___sheep___.
The ___teacher___ told the class to be quiet.

The orange pages support children with practice in the various spelling patterns that make a specific long vowel sound. Explain to children that words sounding the same sometimes can be spelt differently and have different meanings, such as "been" and "bean". For the time filler, remember poetry does not need to rhyme, but you may find children use plenty of rhyming words and will be keen for their poem to rhyme.

14

1. Circle the pictures with the short "ea" sound.

eye head bread feather bird

2. Add the letters **ea** to complete these words. Say the words aloud.

ready heavy thread
weather breakfast health

3. Complete the words with one of these spelling patterns: **eer ear**

cheer hear steer
fear clear deer

15

4. Use the words you made in question 3 to complete the sentences.

The crowd gave a ___cheer___.
Dan could ___hear___ the crowd.
The fish swam in the ___clear___ water.
The people ___fear___ the dragon.
" ___Steer___ the ship to the left," said the captain.
The hikers saw a ___deer___ in the forest.

5. Find these words in the word search.

peer near deadly year already weapon

s	y	e	o	n	w	d
w	e	a	p	o	n	e
e	a	l	y	r	e	a
c	r	d	a	r	a	d
e	a	p	e	e	r	l
a	l	r	e	a	d	y

If children are finding it tricky to decide which pattern to use, encourage them to write down the options and identify visually the correct spelling or use a dictionary to check. Some children may rely on their visual memory of the shape of a word and the pattern of its letters to help them remember how to spell it.

Answers:

16–17 Letter clusters
18–19 Verb endings

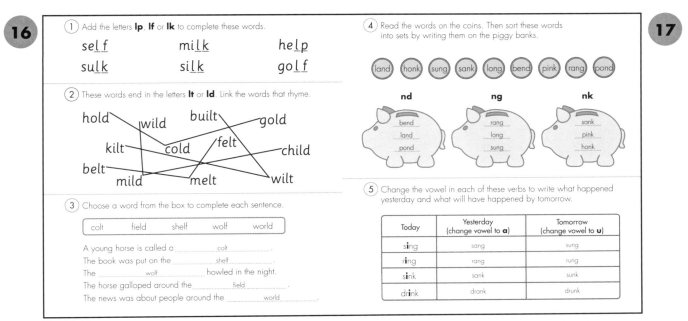

16

1. Add the letters **lp**, **lf** or **lk** to complete these words.

se**lf** mi**lk** he**lp**

su**lk** si**lk** go**lf**

2. These words end in the letters **lt** or **ld**. Link the words that rhyme.

hold wild built gold
kilt cold felt child
belt mild melt wilt

3. Choose a word from the box to complete each sentence.

| colt | field | shelf | wolf | world |

A young horse is called a _____colt_____.
The book was put on the _____shelf_____.
The _____wolf_____ howled in the night.
The horse galloped around the _____field_____.
The news was about people around the _____world_____.

17

4. Read the words on the coins. Then sort these words into sets by writing them on the piggy banks.

(land) (honk) (sung) (sank) (long) (bend) (pink) (rang) (pond)

nd
bend
land
pond

ng
rang
long
sung

nk
sank
pink
honk

5. Change the vowel in each of these verbs to write what happened yesterday and what will have happened by tomorrow.

Today	Yesterday (change vowel to **a**)	Tomorrow (change vowel to **u**)
s**i**ng	sang	sung
r**i**ng	rang	rung
s**i**nk	sank	sunk
dr**i**nk	drank	drunk

The red pages provide many examples to practise how consonants blend together in words. Encourage children to think of other words with blends that contain the letter **l** in them. Also point out to children that sometimes consonants join together to make one sound, such as "ng". Being familiar with alphabetical order will help with using a dictionary, indexes and glossaries.

18

1. Add **-ing** to each verb to tell what is happening now.

shout**ing** lift**ing** cook**ing**

pull**ing** jump**ing** rest**ing**

2. Add **-ed** to each verb to tell what has happened before.

melt**ed** ask**ed** help**ed**

land**ed** climb**ed** look**ed**

3. These verbs end in **e**. Drop the **e** in these verbs before adding **-ing** or **-ed**.

Verb	Happen**ing** now (add **-ing**)	Happen**ed** before (add **-ed**)
use	using	used
bake	baking	baked
hike	hiking	hiked
vote	voting	voted

19

4. Tick (✔) the correct spelling.

marryed or married ✔
cryed or cried ✔
enjoyed ✔ or enjoied

marrying ✔ or marriing
crying ✔ or criing
enjoying ✔ or enjoiing

Write the rule for when a **y** is changed to an **i**.

Only when adding **-ed** and when the verb has a consonant before the **y**

5. These verbs have a short vowel sound. Double the last consonant before adding the verb endings **-ing** and **-ed** to each word.

fit [add **-ing**] → fitting   spot [add **-ed**] → spotted

hum [add **-ing**] → humming   tap [add **-ed**] → tapped

cut [add **-ing**] → cutting   rub [add **-ed**] → rubbed

Make sure your child understands that a verb is an action word. A sentence is made complete by having a verb. The verb ending **-ing** always adds an extra syllable to a word and **-ed** sometimes does. The past tense of some verbs may sound as if they end in "id", "d" or "t", but all these sounds are spelt **ed**.

Answers:

22–23 More clusters
24–25 "er" sound

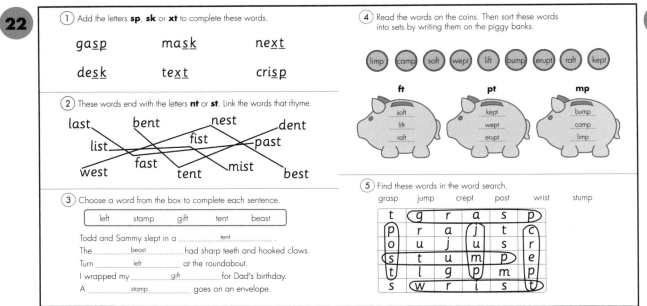

22

① Add the letters **sp**, **sk** or **xt** to complete these words.

ga<u>sp</u>   ma<u>sk</u>   ne<u>xt</u>

de<u>sk</u>   te<u>xt</u>   cri<u>sp</u>

② These words end with the letters **nt** or **st**. Link the words that rhyme.

last   bent   nest   dent
list   fist   past
west   fast   tent   mist   best

③ Choose a word from the box to complete each sentence.

| left | stamp | gift | tent | beast |

Todd and Sammy slept in a _____tent_____ .
The _____beast_____ had sharp teeth and hooked claws.
Turn _____left_____ at the roundabout.
I wrapped my _____gift_____ for Dad's birthday.
A _____stamp_____ goes on an envelope.

23

④ Read the words on the coins. Then sort these words into sets by writing them on the piggy banks.

limp camp soft wept lift bump erupt raft kept

ft
soft
lift
raft

pt
kept
wept
erupt

mp
bump
camp
limp

⑤ Find these words in the word search.

grasp   jump   crept   post   wrist   stump

t	g	r	a	s	p
p	r	a	j	t	c
o	u	j	u	s	r
s	t	u	m	p	e
t	l	g	p	m	p
s	w	r	i	s	t

These pages practise further consonant combinations at the ends of words. There are a variety of activities to reinforce this knowledge in different ways: selecting the correct letters to complete the words, listening for words that rhyme, using the words in the context of a sentence and looking closely for the individual letters that spell a word in a word search.

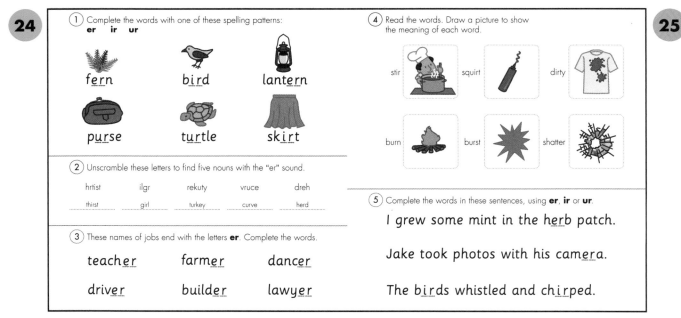

24

① Complete the words with one of these spelling patterns:
er ir ur

f<u>er</u>n   b<u>ir</u>d   lant<u>er</u>n

p<u>ur</u>se   t<u>ur</u>tle   sk<u>ir</u>t

② Unscramble these letters to find five nouns with the "er" sound.

hrtist   ilgr   rekuty   vruce   dreh
thirst   girl   turkey   curve   herd

③ These names of jobs end with the letters **er**. Complete the words.

teach<u>er</u>   farm<u>er</u>   danc<u>er</u>

driv<u>er</u>   build<u>er</u>   lawy<u>er</u>

25

④ Read the words. Draw a picture to show the meaning of each word.

stir   squirt   dirty

burn   burst   shatter

⑤ Complete the words in these sentences, using **er**, **ir** or **ur**.

I grew some mint in the h<u>er</u>b patch.

Jake took photos with his cam<u>er</u>a.

The b<u>ir</u>ds whistled and ch<u>ir</u>ped.

The "er" sound has three common spelling patterns, and children will need to choose the correct pattern. They will either recall other instances of seeing the word or try out options on these pages. If children are struggling to re-organise the letters to form the words, encourage them to find the spelling pattern and then see which letters are left. You could also give them a clue to help identify the word.

Answers:

26–27 Blends and ends
28–29 Compare adjectives

26

1. Look at the pictures. Add the letters **sh** or **ch** to complete the words.

ship   shell   brush
chick   cheese   peach

2. Underline the "th" sound when it appears in these sentences.
Note: There are two "th" sounds as in "then" and in "thistle".

The three brothers were thrilled.

Thunder crashed around them.

Their mother and father were thankful.

27

3. Draw a line to link the words that rhyme.

match — hatch
lunch — munch
fish — dish
catch — match
bunch — lunch
hatch
cash — dash
dash — cash
wish — fish
sash — cash
munch — bunch
dish — wish

4. Change the vowel sound to make a new word from each of these words. Use **a, e, i, o** or **u**. Answers may vary.

think	shop	rush	bench	hutch
thank	ship	rash	bunch	hatch

5. Complete these words using the letters **shr** or **thr**.

throne   shrub   throb
shrimp   throat   shriek

The letter combinations on these pages make a single sound and are known as digraphs. Tongue twisters are a fun way of becoming familiar with saying the sounds at the beginning and end of words. Extend the time filler activity further by asking children to identify the words that rhyme and to note how they are spelt using different letter combinations.

28

1. Add **-er** to each word to compare two things.

faster   richer   weaker
slower   poorer   stronger

2. Add **-est** to each word to mean the top thing.

oldest   lowest   shortest
youngest   highest   tallest

3. These words have a short vowel sound. Double the last consonant before adding the endings.

Adjective	Compare two things (add -er)	The top things (add -est)
fit	fitter	fittest
thin	thinner	thinnest
hot	hotter	hottest
wet	wetter	wettest

29

4. These words end in **e** or **y**. Drop the **e** or change the **y** to an **i** in these words before adding **-er** or **-est**.

nice (add -er) → nicer
pretty (add -est) → prettiest
wide (add -er) → wider
large (add -est) → largest
heavy (add -er) → heavier
tiny (add -est) → tiniest

5. Some adjectives do not follow the rules. Use these words to complete the chart.

little   better   worst   many   most   less

Adjective	Compare two things	The top things
good	better	best
little	less	least
bad	worse	worst
many	more	most

Check that children know that an adjective is a word that describes a person, place or thing. As with the work on adding verb endings (see page 18), there are additional rules to know when adding these adjective endings to words with a short vowel sound or that end in **e** or **y**. Children need to be aware of the words that do not follow the rules. Help children by suggesting sentences that these words are used in.

Answers:

30–31 Long "i" sound
32–33 Beginning blends

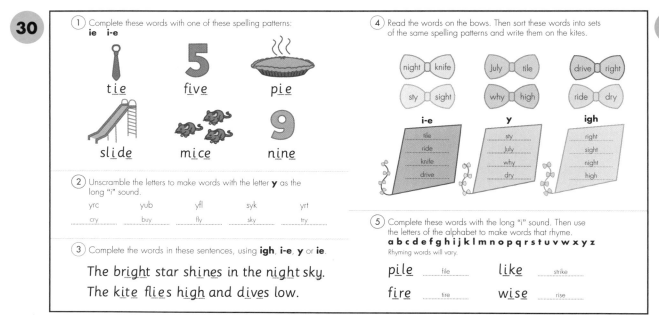

30

① Complete these words with one of these spelling patterns:
ie   i-e

t**ie**   f**i**ve   p**ie**

sl**i**de   m**i**ce   n**i**ne

② Unscramble the letters to make words with the letter **y** as the long "i" sound.

yrc	yub	yfl	syk	yrt
cry	buy	fly	sky	try

③ Complete the words in these sentences, using **igh**, **i-e**, **y** or **ie**.

The br**igh**t star sh**i**nes in the n**igh**t sky.

The k**i**te fl**ie**s h**igh** and d**i**ves low.

31

④ Read the words on the bows. Then sort these words into sets of the same spelling patterns and write them on the kites.

night | knife   July | tile   drive | right

sty | sight   why | high   ride | dry

i-e
tile
ride
knife
drive

y
sty
July
why
dry

igh
right
sight
night
high

⑤ Complete these words with the long "i" sound. Then use the letters of the alphabet to make words that rhyme.
a b c d e f g h i j k l m n o p q r s t u v w x y z
Rhyming words will vary.

p**i**le   file   l**i**ke   strike

f**i**re   tire   w**i**se   rise

The long "i" sound has four common spelling patterns: **ie**, **i** + final **e**, **igh** and the letter **y**. Answers will vary for the rhymes for question 5. The answers do not need to use the same spelling pattern, for example "pies" as a rhyme for "wise". The first step to writing a poem is to compile a list of words to use. Encourage your child to read their poem aloud.

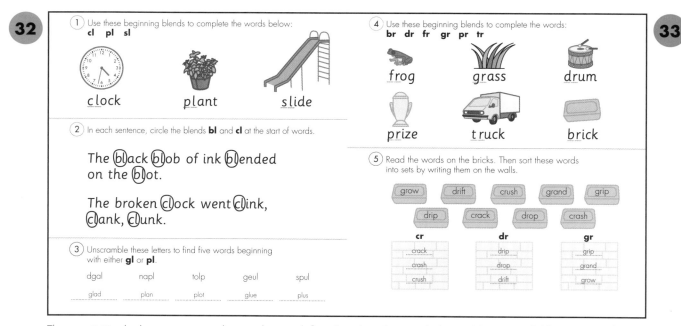

32

① Use these beginning blends to complete the words below:
cl   pl   sl

clock   **pl**ant   **sl**ide

② In each sentence, circle the blends **bl** and **cl** at the start of words.

The ⓑlack ⓑlob of ink ⓑlended on the ⓑlot.

The broken ⓒlock went ⓒlink, ⓒlank, ⓒlunk.

③ Unscramble these letters to find five words beginning with either **gl** or **pl**.

dgal	napl	tolp	geul	spul
glad	plan	plot	glue	plus

33

④ Use these beginning blends to complete the words:
br   dr   fr   gr   pr   tr

frog   **gr**ass   **dr**um

prize   **tr**uck   **br**ick

⑤ Read the words on the bricks. Then sort these words into sets by writing them on the walls.

grow | drift | crush | grand | grip

drip | crack | drop | crash

cr
crack
crash
crush

dr
drip
drop
drift

gr
grip
grand
grow

These activities look at consonants that combine with **l** and **r** at the beginning of words to create a blend. Encourage children to read aloud or repeat after you the sentences in question 2. The time filler suggests a fun game that can be played out and about. When your child is more confident, this game can be developed by the letters having to be used in the same order or competing with others to see who can think of the longest word using the letters.

Answers:

34–35 Contractions
36–37 Long "o" sound

34

1) Separate each word into two words.

he's	he is
you'll	you will
didn't	did not
I've	I have

2) Combine the two words to make one word in each case.

can not	can't
you are	you're
she will	she'll
we have	we've

3) Match each pair of words to its contraction.

could not — couldn't
do not — don't
I am — I'm
it is — it's

35

4) For each sentence, circle the two words that can be combined. Write the contraction.

(Who is) coming to see the movie? — Who's

(You are) going to be late for the show. — You're

(What is) on today? — What's

(We have) been to the cinema. — We've

5) Tick (✔) the correct sentences and put a cross (✗) against an error. Then correct the mistakes.

"Where's your book?" asked the teacher. ✔

"Its at home," said Emma. ✗ It's

She'ad forgotten it. ✗ She'd

"I'll bring it in tomorrow," she said. ✔

Through reading, speaking and listening, children will learn that sometimes two words are joined together and shortened with letters left out. These are called contractions.

An apostrophe is used to indicate where the letter or letters have been taken out. This often happens with words next to pronouns, such as "I", "we" and "you".

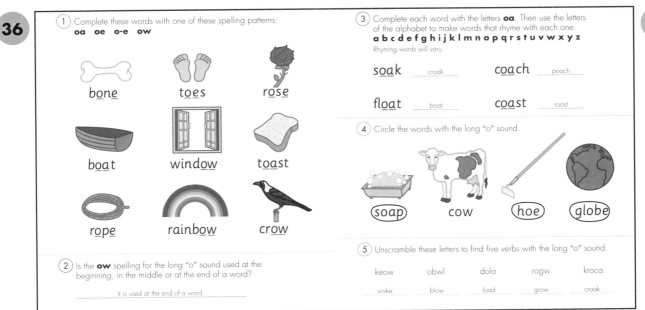

36

1) Complete these words with one of these spelling patterns:
oa oe o-e ow

bone   toes   rose

boat   window   toast

rope   rainbow   crow

2) Is the **ow** spelling for the long "o" sound used at the beginning, in the middle or at the end of a word?

It is used at the end of a word.

37

3) Complete each word with the letters **oa**. Then use the letters of the alphabet to make words that rhyme with each one.
a b c d e f g h i j k l m n o p q r s t u v w x y z
Rhyming words will vary.

soak — croak   coach — poach

float — boat   coast — roast

4) Circle the words with the long "o" sound.

(soap)   cow   (hoe)   (globe)

5) Unscramble these letters to find five verbs with the long "o" sound.

keow	obwl	dola	rogw	kroca
woke	blow	load	grow	croak

There are four common spelling patterns for the long "o" sound. As spelling is tricky, splitting words into sound chunks or learning a phrase or rhyme using the letters in the word is a helpful tool to use. There are a number of examples in the time fillers throughout this book. Encourage children to think of their own for words they are finding tricky to spell.

Answers:

38–39 "oy" and "ow" sounds
40–41 Tricky blends

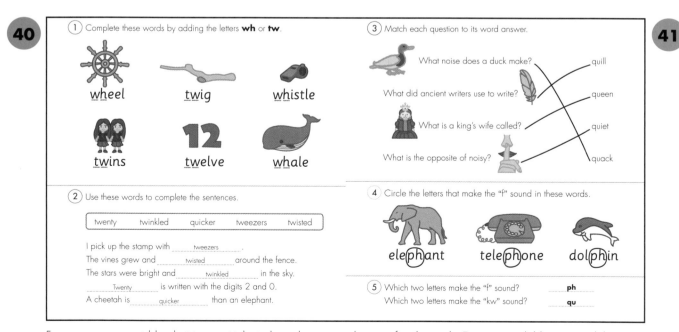

38

1) Circle the pictures with the "oy" and "ow" sounds.

2) Add the letters **oi** to complete these words. Say the words aloud.

boil   point   noisy

coin   voice   soil

3) Complete these words with one of these spelling patterns:
oi   oy

join   toy   enjoy

annoy   choice   royal

39

4) Complete each word with the letters **ou** or **ow**. Then use the letters of the alphabet to make words that rhyme with each one.
a b c d e f g h i j k l m n o p q r s t u v w x y z
Rhyming words will vary.

crown ..... gown   allow ..... now

mouth ..... south   cloud ..... loud

howl ..... owl   house ..... mouse

flower ..... flour   found ..... ground

5) Use these words to complete the sentences below.

| loud | down | mouse | outside | crowd |

The ..... crowd ..... gave a cheer and waved flags.
The music was very ..... loud ..... at the concert.
A lady screamed when she saw a ..... mouse ..... .
The people went ..... down ..... the stairs.
When it started to rain ..... outside ..... , everyone ran inside.

These pages cover two separate sounds "oy" as in "boy" and "ow" as in "crown". There are two common spelling patterns for each sound: **oy** and **oi** for "oy" sound; and **ow** and **ou** for the "ow" sound. Remind children that the letters **ow** can also make the long "o" sound as practised on page 37.

40

1) Complete these words by adding the letters **wh** or **tw**.

wheel   twig   whistle

twins   twelve   whale

2) Use these words to complete the sentences.

| twenty | twinkled | quicker | tweezers | twisted |

I pick up the stamp with ..... tweezers ..... .
The vines grew and ..... twisted ..... around the fence.
The stars were bright and ..... twinkled ..... in the sky.
..... Twenty ..... is written with the digits 2 and 0.
A cheetah is ..... quicker ..... than an elephant.

41

3) Match each question to its word answer.

What noise does a duck make?   quill

What did ancient writers use to write?   queen

What is a king's wife called?   quiet

What is the opposite of noisy?   quack

4) Circle the letters that make the "f" sound in these words.

ele**ph**ant   tele**ph**one   dol**ph**in

5) Which two letters make the "f" sound?   **ph**
   Which two letters make the "kw" sound?   **qu**

For some consonant blends it is very tricky to hear the letters, such as **wh**, and for some, such as **qu** and **ph**, there are no clues in the sound they make. Remind your child that the letter **q** is always followed by **u** in the words they are familiar with. Encourage children to read the words once they have completed the page to reinforce further the spelling–sound connections.

Answers:

42–43 Plurals
46–47 "or" sound

42

1. Most words are made plural by adding an **s**, but there are exceptions. If the ending has an extra syllable, then add **-es**. Write the plural forms for these words.

cat — cats   box — boxes
rock — rocks   glass — glasses

2. Tick (✔) the spelling that is right.

✔ valleys or valleies   ✔ ladys or ladies
✔ citys or cities   ✔ pennys or pennies
✔ keys or keies   ✔ chimneys or chimneies

Write the rule for when a **y** is changed to an **i**.
Only when the word has a consonant before the **y**

3. If a word ends in an "f" sound, change the **f** to a **v** and add **-es**. Write the plural forms for these words.

knife — knives   shelf — shelves   calf — calves   leaf — leaves

43

4. Make the words plural by adding **-s** or **-es**. Check in a dictionary.

kangaroo — kangaroos   piano — pianos
hero — heroes   tomato — tomatoes
potato — potatoes   volcano — volcanoes

5. Some words change completely from the singular to the plural form. Match each word to its correct plural.

goose → geese
tooth → teeth
child → children
mouse → mice

Check that children know the term "plural" refers to more than one thing. By now, they should know that some plurals can be made by adding the letter **s**. However, depending on the singular word, an **es** may be added or letters be altered before adding an **s** or **es**. These pages practise these rules and provide some exceptions.

46

1. Complete these words with one of these spelling patterns: **or oar oor ore**

horn   score   fork   roar   door   oar

2. Unscramble these letters to find five words with the "or" sound.

arro — roar   reom — more   norb — born   trof — fort   rlofo — floor

3. Complete these words with the spelling patterns **au** or **aw**.

claw   shawl   author   pawprint   straw   saucer

47

4. Find these words in the word search.

board   wore   crawl   sport   north   dawn

t	w	d	c	s	n
b	o	a	r	d	o
o	r	w	a	s	r
s	e	n	w	p	t
t	h	g	l	m	h
s	p	o	r	t	t

5. Use these words to complete the sentences below.

haunted   drawer   fork   corners

Everybody was scared to go into the haunted house.
A triangle has three corners
Liz put away her shirts in the top drawer
His fork slipped off his plate.

These pages might be challenging as the activities require them to practise the many spelling possibilities for the "or" sound. Point out that the letters **au** never come at the ends of words, so for words like "straw" and compound words like "pawprint", the letters **aw** are used.

Answers:

48–49 More beginning blends
50–51 Long "oo" sound

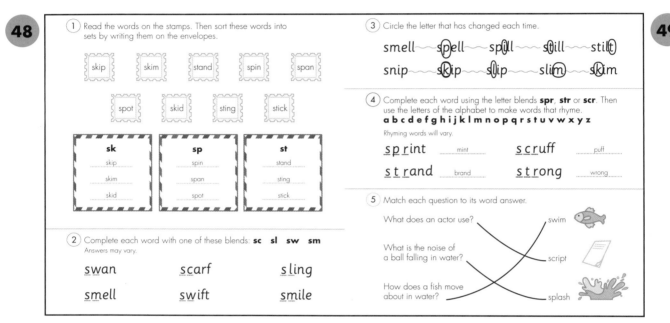

48

1) Read the words on the stamps. Then sort these words into sets by writing them on the envelopes.

skip   skim   stand   spin   span

spot   skid   sting   stick

sk	sp	st
skip	spin	stand
skim	span	sting
skid	spot	stick

2) Complete each word with one of these blends: **sc sl sw sm**
Answers may vary.

swan   scarf   sling

smell   swift   smile

49

3) Circle the letter that has changed each time.

smell — s(p)ell — sp(i)ll — s(t)ill — stil(t)
snip — sk(k)ip — s(l)ip — sli(m) — sk(i)m

4) Complete each word using the letter blends **spr**, **str** or **scr**. Then use the letters of the alphabet to make words that rhyme.
a b c d e f g h i j k l m n o p q r s t u v w x y z
Rhyming words will vary.

s p rint ___ mint   s c ruff ___ puff
s t rand ___ brand   s t rong ___ wrong

5) Match each question to its word answer.

What does an actor use?   swim
What is the noise of a ball falling in water?   script
How does a fish move about in water?   splash

Support your child in reading aloud the words on these pages as he/she will then hear how the sound has been made by the blends. For question 2, there are a few options for answers for some of these words, e.g., "scan", "swan", "sling" or "swing". Praise your child if he/she notices this and discuss the meanings of the different words.

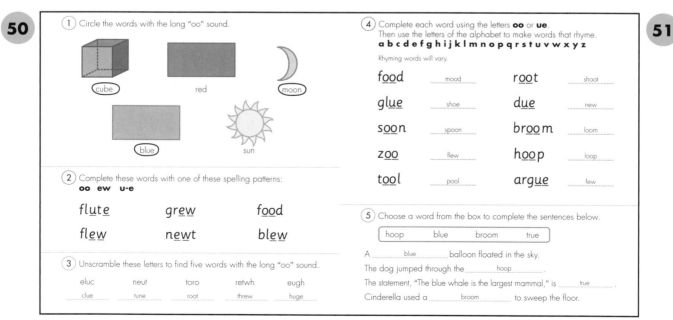

50

1) Circle the words with the long "oo" sound.

cube   red   moon

blue   sun

2) Complete these words with one of these spelling patterns:
oo ew u-e

flute   grew   food
flew   newt   blew

3) Unscramble these letters to find five words with the long "oo" sound.

eluc   neut   toro   retwh   eugh
clue   tune   root   threw   huge

51

4) Complete each word using the letters **oo** or **ue**. Then use the letters of the alphabet to make words that rhyme.
a b c d e f g h i j k l m n o p q r s t u v w x y z
Rhyming words will vary.

f oo d ___ mood   r oo t ___ shoot
gl ue ___ shoe   d ue ___ new
s oo n ___ spoon   br oo m ___ loom
z oo ___ flew   h oo p ___ loop
t oo l ___ pool   arg ue ___ few

5) Choose a word from the box to complete the sentences below.

hoop	blue	broom	true

A ___ blue ___ balloon floated in the sky.
The dog jumped through the ___ hoop ___.
The statement, "The blue whale is the largest mammal," is ___ true ___.
Cinderella used a ___ broom ___ to sweep the floor.

The long "oo" sound can also be known as the long "u" sound. The sound is represented by a number of spelling patterns that are useful for children to know. Point out that the letters **oo** are rarely used at the ends of words but **ew** often does. For question 3, first find the letters for the spelling pattern and then fit the other letters around it.

Answers:

52-53 Short "oo" sound
54-55 Silent letters

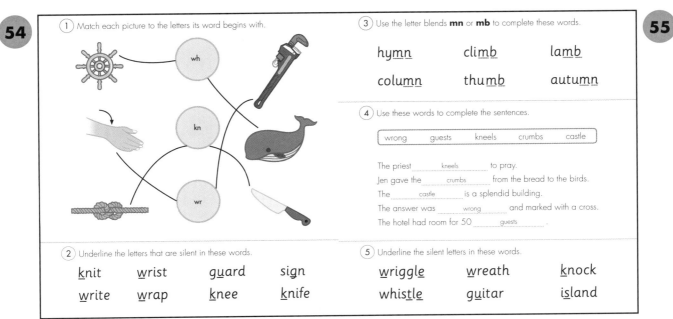

52

1. The letters **oo** are used to spell two different sounds. Circle the pictures with the short **oo** sound.

2. Complete these words with the **oo** spelling.

look   stood   wood

brook   took   wool

3. Write a sentence for each of these words.

could   _____ Answers will vary. _____

should   _____ Answers will vary. _____

would   _____ Answers will vary. _____

53

4. Find these words in the word search.

shook   hood   good   cook   soot
brook   foot   wood   crook   book

s	g	c	a	z	i	e
h	o	o	d	f	c	y
o	o	o	u	o	r	p
o	d	k	w	o	o	d
k	s	o	o	t	o	q
j	b	r	o	o	k	a
b	o	o	k	w	e	m

5. Use the letter **u** to make the short "oo" sound in each word.

pull   push   sugar

bush   full   bull

All the spelling patterns for this short "oo" sound, such as in "push", are used for other sounds too. Check that children are able to hear the difference between the long and short "oo" sounds in the first question. The words in question 3 are very useful and children should be encouraged to learn them.

54

1. Match each picture to the letters its word begins with.

wh

kn

wr

2. Underline the letters that are silent in these words.

knit   wrist   guard   sign

write   wrap   knee   knife

55

3. Use the letter blends **mn** or **mb** to complete these words.

hymn   climb   lamb

column   thumb   autumn

4. Use these words to complete the sentences.

wrong   guests   kneels   crumbs   castle

The priest _____ kneels _____ to pray.
Jen gave the _____ crumbs _____ from the bread to the birds.
The _____ castle _____ is a splendid building.
The answer was _____ wrong _____ and marked with a cross.
The hotel had room for 50 _____ guests _____ .

5. Underline the silent letters in these words.

wriggle   wreath   knock

whistle   guitar   island

Children need to be aware and watch out for letters that can't be clearly heard in a word, often referred to as silent. The letters featured on this page are some of the most common ones: **kn**, **gu**, **mn**, **mb** and **wr**.

Point out when words with these silent letters appear in the material children read. Continue to check that children know how to spell the days of the week, as "Wednesday" is not the only tricky one to spell.

(78)

Answers:

56–57 Prefixes and suffixes
58–59 The letter **y**

56

1) Add the prefix **un-** to the beginning of each of these words.

un**happy** un**do** un**load**

un**fair** un**lock** un**well**

What do you think the prefix **un-** means? not

2) Add the suffix **-less** to the ends of these words.

hope**less** rest**less** end**less**

tire**less** speech**less** age**less**

What do you think the suffix **-less** means? without

3) Complete these words.

enjoy + ment = enjoyment   sad + ness = sadness

punish + ment = punishment   fit + ness = fitness

agree + ment = agreement   dark + ness = darkness

pay + ment = payment   ill + ness = illness

57

4) Add the suffix **-ful** to the ends of these words.

use**ful** cheer**ful** pain**ful**

wonder**ful** care**ful** mind**ful**

What do you think the suffix **-ful** means? full of

5) Combine a word from the red box with a word part from the green box to make 10 new words.

| joy | play | glad | open | help | power | cover |

| un- | -less | -ful | -ness |

Count the syllables for each of your new words.

joyful 2   unopen 3
helpless 2   helpful 2
gladness 2   powerful 3
uncover 3   powerless 3
openness 3   playful 2

Children are introduced to common prefixes and suffixes in Year 2. Knowing about these parts added to the beginning and ends of words will help children break down long words into manageable chunks to spell. Also, explain to children how prefixes and suffixes can alter the meanings of words, such as "endless" means to be without an end.

58

1) The letter **y** sometimes makes a long "e" sound at the end of a word. Add a **y** to complete these words.

baby   family   honey

2) The letter **y** makes a long "i" sound when there are no other vowels in the word. Unscramble these letters to make words.

kys   yhw   rcy   ylf   ryf
sky   why   cry   fly   fry

3) Tick (✔) in the correct box to show what sound the **y** makes.

Word	Long "e" sound	Long "i" sound
body	✔	
type		✔
empty	✔	
shy		✔

59

4) The letter **y** can also make a long "a" sound and a short "i" sound. Find these words in the word search.

prey cylinder pyramid syrup crystal myth gym

s	p	h	t	g	y	m	c
c	y	l	i	n	d	e	r
p	r	e	y	u	t	s	y
d	a	y	m	a	h	p	s
l	m	s	y	r	u	p	t
y	i	p	t	h	a	y	a
c	d	l	h	t	y	g	l

5) For plurals, if the **y** follows a consonant, then change the **y** to an **i** and add **-es**. Tick (✔) the correct plural.

babys or ✔ babies   ✔ monkeys or monkeies

✔ trays or traies   familys or ✔ families

These activities demonstrate how even one letter can have two or more different sounds. Question 5 provides further practice in changing the **y** to an **i** before adding endings. A spelling diary suggested in the time filler will be a useful resource for children if they record words they are finding tricky to spell. The pages could follow the content covered in this book.

Answers:

60–61 "j" and "l" sounds
62–63 Homophones and homographs

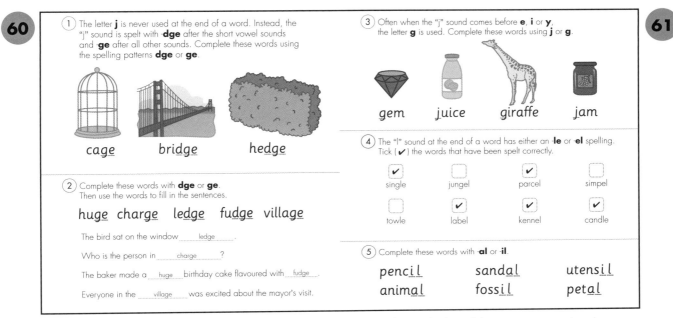

60

① The letter **j** is never used at the end of a word. Instead, the "j" sound is spelt with **-dge** after the short vowel sounds and **-ge** after all other sounds. Complete these words using the spelling patterns **dge** or **ge**.

cage   bridge   hedge

② Complete these words with **dge** or **ge**. Then use the words to fill in the sentences.

huge   charge   ledge   fudge   village

The bird sat on the window ___ledge___ .

Who is the person in ___charge___ ?

The baker made a ___huge___ birthday cake flavoured with ___fudge___ .

Everyone in the ___village___ was excited about the mayor's visit.

61

③ Often when the "j" sound comes before **e**, **i** or **y**, the letter **g** is used. Complete these words using **j** or **g**.

gem   juice   giraffe   jam

④ The "l" sound at the end of a word has either an **-le** or **-el** spelling. Tick (✔) the words that have been spelt correctly.

✔ single   ☐ jungel   ✔ parcel   ☐ simpel

☐ towle   ✔ label   ✔ kennel   ✔ candle

⑤ Complete these words with **-al** or **-il**.

pencil   sandal   utensil
animal   fossil   petal

These pages show that even some consonant sounds have more than one spelling pattern. The "j" sound made when using the letter **g** can also be known as the soft "g" sound.

This time filler is the last of the activities to make other words from the letters of a long word. If children have enjoyed these, encourage them to try out other words.

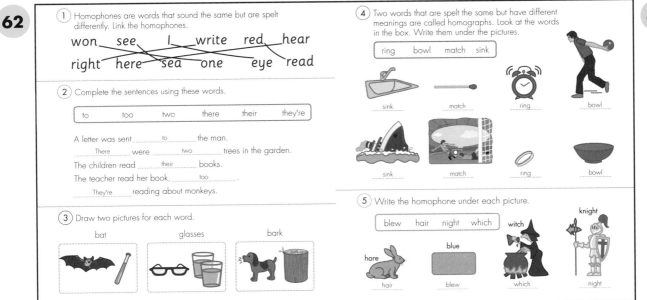

62

① Homophones are words that sound the same but are spelt differently. Link the homophones.

won   see   I   write   red   hear
right   here   sea   one   eye   read

② Complete the sentences using these words.

to   too   two   there   their   they're

A letter was sent ___to___ the man.
___There___ were ___two___ trees in the garden.
The children read ___their___ books.
The teacher read her book, ___too___ .
___They're___ reading about monkeys.

③ Draw two pictures for each word.

bat   glasses   bark

63

④ Two words that are spelt the same but have different meanings are called homographs. Look at the words in the box. Write them under the pictures.

ring   bowl   match   sink

sink   match   ring   bowl

sink   match   ring   bowl

⑤ Write the homophone under each picture.

blew   hair   night   which

witch   knight

hare   blue

hair   blew   which   night

Homophones are words that sound the same but are spelt differently. Homographs are words that are spelt the same but have different meanings. Extend the activity by asking children to put the words into sentences. Children could start a homophone and homograph list and add words as they come across them in their reading and conversation.

Answers:

200 words useful to learn to spell

This list of 200 key words for your child to learn to spell includes the words on the Useful word lists on pages 20–21, 44–45 and 64–65. Encourage your child to learn these words by looking and saying each word aloud, then covering the word and writing it and then checking. Encourage children to say/write sentences using the words. Once your child is familiar with each group of 10 words then test her/him regularly.

he	can	the	from	left	gave	time	hand	red	January
she	say	that	get	right	give	sing	head	black	February
him	said	they	about	last	live	read	help	blue	March
his	with	their	back	first	long	call	home	white	April
her	want	them	been	second	bring	eat	house	green	May
you	was	then	before	third	best	work	never	brown	June
me	will	this	after	fast	boy	wish	next	yellow	July
my	well	there	again	slow	girl	play	once	grey	August
are	went	these	away	like	round	don't	open	purple	September
for	were	three	always	little	good	can't	close	orange	October
have	one	made	out	soon	any	sit	could	Monday	November
has	two	make	only	stop	many	walk	should	Tuesday	December
had	did	more	often	start	ask	run	would	Wednesday	month
here	do	much	over	take	put	jump	very	Thursday	year
came	down	why	under	tell	pull	skip	every	Friday	school
come	up	where	must	fell	push	climb	other	Saturday	rain
some	so	when	just	find	than	tree	another	Sunday	cloud
see	no	which	your	found	thing	bird	because	today	snow
saw	new	who	old	four	think	animal	yes	tomorrow	wind
how	now	what	own	five	thought	fish	going	yesterday	weather